CGP

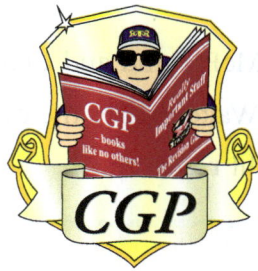

Problem Solving & Reasoning Activity Book

for ages 9-10

This CGP book is bursting with fun activities to build up children's skills and confidence.

It's ideal for extra practice to reinforce what they're learning in primary school. Enjoy!

Published by CGP

Editors:
Ruth Greenhalgh, Jake McGuffie, Sean McParland and Claire Plowman

With thanks to Alison Griffin and Julie Wakeling for the proofreading.

With thanks to Jade Sim for the copyright research.

ISBN: 978 1 83774 067 3

Printed by Elanders Ltd, Newcastle upon Tyne.
Clipart on the cover and throughout the book from Corel®
Cover design concept by emc design ltd.

Contents

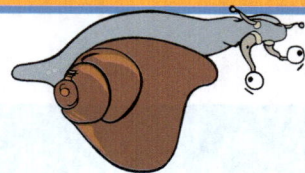

Working with Numbers

Numbers can have lots of different digits, and you've got to know them all:

millions
hundreds
tens
ones
thousandths
hundred thousands
ten thousands
thousands
tenths
hundredths

$$7\ 120\ 943\ .\ 586$$

You round decimals in the same way as whole numbers. E.g. to round to one decimal place, look at the second decimal place. If it's less than 5, round down. If it's 5 or more, round up.

1 d.p.   2 d.p.

So, rounding 3.58 to 1 d.p. gives 3.6, because 8 is 5 or more.

You can use a number line to help you count forwards and backwards with positive and negative numbers.

Count forward 5 places to get from −3 to 2.

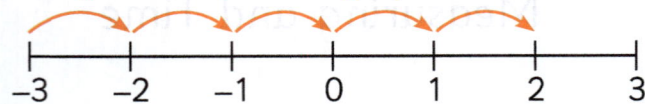

−3   −2   −1   0   1   2   3

A **power of ten** is a number that's a 1 followed by zeros, e.g. 10, 100, 1000 or 10 000. So counting up in a power of ten just means adding that power of ten each step. E.g.:

To count up in 1000s, add 1 to the thousands digit each time.

+ 1000   + 1000   + 1000

12 670   13 670   14 670   15 670

Now Try These

1. Paolo partitions 98 345 in the following way, but he makes a mistake.

   98 345   =   92 300   +   6200   +   120   +   20   +   5

   What number should replace 6200 to make the partition correct?

   ....

2. Cross out the number that rounds (to 1 d.p.) to a different number from the rest.

   9.42   9.38   9.44   9.34

   9.35

2

3. Fill in the gaps in the sequence below by counting in equal steps of a power of ten.

| 58 816 | .... | .... | .... | 59 216 |

4. Flo works in a pastry kitchen. The temperature of her butter is 4 °C.
She puts it in the freezer until it gets 8 °C cooler, then takes it out.
The butter then gets 3 °C warmer.

a) What temperature is Flo's butter now?

.... °C

b) The temperature of her cake is 8 °C,
rounded to the nearest whole number.
What is the lowest temperature the cake could be?

.... °C

5. The maximum scores on the levels in a video game go up in equal steps.
To fight the final boss, you need to score 250 000 on a level.
What is the first level you can fight the final boss on?

| 150 000 | → | 160 000 | → | 170 000 | → | 180 000 | → | ... |
| Level 1 | | Level 2 | | Level 3 | | Level 4 | | |

Level ....

An Extra Challenge

Take a look at this diary extract from Iva the Diver's latest plunge.
Can you work out how deep below sea level (0 m) she went?

My initial dive took me to −121 m.
I went 10 m further down and saw
jellyfish, so I went back up 30 m.
Afterwards, I went down 3 m
more, then 50 m more — only to
find sharks! Then I called it a day.

Did you make easy work
of these numbers?

3

Adding and Subtracting

How It Works

Some problems will need you to add and subtract at different stages.
Here's an example of this sort of problem:

> Over a great many years, the Kingdom of Throwalot has produced hundreds of world-class shot putters. Between them all, they have earned 25 497 medals. 12 400 of the medals are bronze, 8 532 are silver and the rest are gold. How many gold medals do the shot putters have between them?

Step 1: Addition

Add together the number of bronze and silver medals.

```
  12400
+  8532
-------
  20932
   1
```

Step 2: Subtraction

```
    4 14
  2 5̸ 4̸ 9 7
-  2 0 9 3 2
-----------
      4 5 6 5
```

Subtract this from the overall total to find the number of gold medals.

(The column method works for decimal numbers too, if you line up the decimal points.)

Check your answers by rounding, e.g. to the nearest thousand:

12 000 + 9 000 = 21 000   25 000 − 21 000 = 4 000

Now Try These

1. Fill in the missing numbers in the calculations below.

```
   1 5 3 □ 0 4
+  □ 9 1 2 3 4
-------------
   5 □ 5 1 3 □
   1     1
```

```
            □ 13
   8 6 5 6̸ 3̸ 7
-  7 0 1 □ □ 6
-------------
   □ 6 4 0 6 1
```

2. At a football match, there are 64 798 home fans and 12 989 away fans.
   Isabel estimates there are 82 000 fans at the match in total.
   Use rounding to find a better estimate than Isabel's.
   Write down your calculation.

....

3. Dr Shrinko wants to be as small as his pet rat, Trisha. Yesterday, he shrunk himself to 34.95 cm tall, but today he is 15.51 cm smaller than that. Trisha is 9.2 cm tall — how much smaller is she than Dr Shrinko today?

.... cm

4. Each year, the number of hot dogs Chef Minnie cooks goes up by the same amount. Two years ago, she cooked 13 412 hot dogs, and last year she cooked 24 670. How many hot dogs will she cook this year?

....

5. A team of four runners complete a relay race and record their lap times. Each runner's lap time is shown below, but one of them is missing. If the team's total time is 59 seconds, what is the fourth runner's lap time?

FINISH

.... s

13.46 s

15.19 s

14.75 s

An Extra Challenge

Intergalactic Airways run a popular space travel business across the galaxy. Can you use their flight records to work out how many passengers travelled with them in each of these four years?

The first record shows the total number of passengers for the year 2123, and the rest show the difference from the previous year.

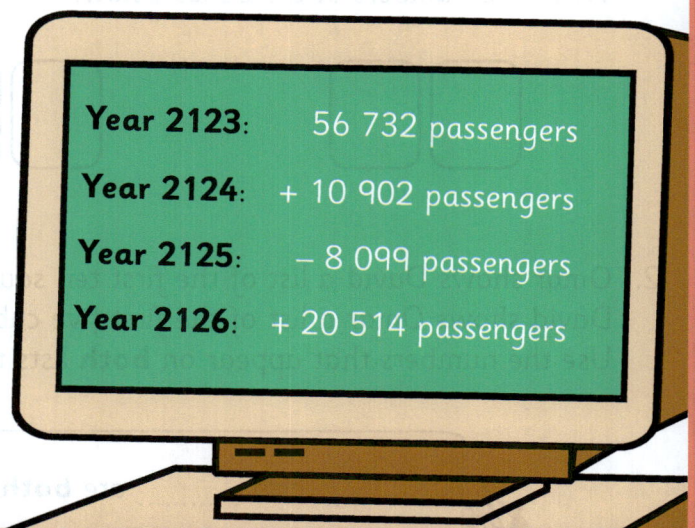

Year 2123:   56 732 passengers

Year 2124:   + 10 902 passengers

Year 2125:   − 8 099 passengers

Year 2126:   + 20 514 passengers

Are you totally happy?
Is anything not adding up?

Factors, Multiples & Primes

How It Works

A **multiple** of a number is just that number multiplied by another whole number.

$3 \times 4 = 12$ ...so 12 is a multiple of 3 and 4.

The **factors** of a number are all the whole numbers that divide it exactly.

$12 \div 3 = 4$

$12 \div 4 = 3$

Since $3 \times 4 = 12$, 3 and 4 are a **factor pair** of 12.

If two numbers share a factor, it's called a **common factor**.

$15 \div 3 = 5$

3 is also a factor of 15, so it is a common factor of 12 and 15.

A **prime number** only has two factors — 1 and itself. Factors that are prime are called... yup, **prime factors**.

3 is prime, because its only factors are 1 and 3. It's a prime factor of 12 and 15.

A **square number** is made by multiplying a number by itself. A **cube number** is made by multiplying a number by itself twice.

$2 \times 2 = 4$ ...so 4 is 2 squared (2^2).

$2 \times 2 \times 2 = 8$ ...so 8 is 2 cubed (2^3).

Now Try These

1. Use each digit card once to make three numbers that are multiples of 9. Write the numbers in the boxes below.

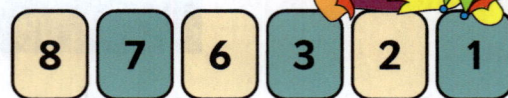

    | 8 | 7 | 6 | 3 | 2 | 1 |

2. Omar shows David a list of the first ten square numbers. David shows Omar a list of the first five cube numbers. Use the numbers that appear on **both** lists to complete the sentence.

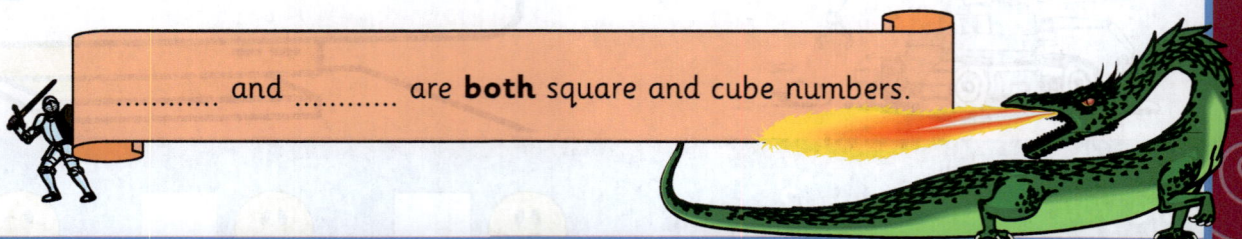

    .... and .... are **both** square and cube numbers.

3. a) Cross out the number that is not a common factor of 60 and 90, then write the missing common factor in the box.

| 1 | 2 | 3 | 5 | 6 | 10 | 12 | 30 | .... |

   b) What are the prime factors of the missing number?

   ....

4. Miguel is going shopping for a lovely factor tree to put in his garden.
   Factor trees have a number at the top, which gets split into a factor pair.
   The numbers keep getting split until only primes are left at the bottom.
   Only one of these factor trees is correct. Circle the correct one.

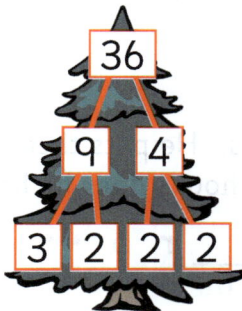

A   B   C   D

An Extra Challenge

The **Factor Tractor 2000** has completely run out of fuel.
Can you work out how many litres
of fuel it needs to fill back up again?

Factor Tractor 2000 fuel instructions:
The number of litres needed is...

1. More than 4 but less than 150
2. 1 less than a square number
3. A multiple of 3
4. A factor of 126

Can you handle primes, whatever the time?

7

Multiplying and Dividing

How It Works

You need to be up to speed on your **times tables** before tackling any multiplying and dividing problems — and make sure you know how by to multiply and divide by **10**, **100** and **1000** too. You also need to be able to use **written methods** — here's how they work:

a) There are 32 tins of paint in a shop. Each tin contains 1473 ml of paint. How much paint is there in the shop in total?

Use long multiplication to find 32 lots of 1473 ml.

Multiply 1473 by 2.

Then multiply 1473 by 30.

Add the results together to get **47 136 ml** in total.

$$
\begin{array}{r}
1473 \\
\times\ \ \ \ 32 \\
\hline
2946 \\
\scriptstyle 1 \\
44190 \\
\scriptstyle 1\ 2 \\
\hline
47136 \\
\scriptstyle 1\ 1
\end{array}
$$

b) The shopkeeper has 2574 picture hooks. He puts them into bags, with 8 hooks in each bag. How many hooks does he have left over?

Use short division to divide 2574 by 8.

$$8\overline{)2\ {}^2 5\ {}^1 7\ {}^1 4} = 0\ 3\ 2\ 1 \ \mathbf{r}\ 6$$

The answer is 321 remainder 6, which means there are **6 hooks** left over (and 321 bags of hooks).

Now Try These

1. A school buys 1000 pencils. The pencils come in packs of 10 and each pack costs £2.85. How much does the school pay for the pencils in total?

    £ ....

2. Fill in the missing numbers in these sentences.

    a) 12 identical bars of chocolate weigh 1080 g.

        So 1 bar of chocolate weighs .... g.

    b) 90 identical bikes weigh 720 kg.

        So 1 bike weighs .... kg.

3. The gardeners at a stately home are creating a rose garden.
They have 1652 rose plants. They want to plant the roses
in rows, with up to 9 rose plants in each row.

What is the smallest number of rows they can plant?

.... rows

4. At a factory, a T-shirt is made
every 42 seconds. How many
seconds does it take to make
2618 T-shirts? Show your working.

5. Alesha runs 3924 m every day.
How many metres does she run in
two weeks? Show your working.

.... seconds

.... m

An Extra Challenge

Martina makes and sells jewellery. She says:

Beads come in bags of 500. I bought 12 bags of beads.

I used 70 beads to make a necklace.

I used the rest to make bracelets, with 8 beads on each bracelet.

How many bracelets did Martina make? How many beads did she have left over?

Can you solve any multiplying or dividing problem?

🙁 ☐   🙂 ☐   😉 ☐

Fractions, Decimals & Percentages

How It Works

You'll need a few different skills for these problems:

To add or subtract fractions, you need to put them over the same denominator. $\longrightarrow$ $\dfrac{11}{12} - \dfrac{1}{3} = \dfrac{11}{12} - \dfrac{4}{12} = \dfrac{7}{12}$

To multiply a fraction by a whole number, multiply by the numerator and divide by the denominator (in the order that's easiest to do).

$\dfrac{2}{7} \times 28$ $\quad 28 \div 7 = 4$ $\quad 4 \times 2 = 8$ $\quad$ So $\dfrac{2}{7} \times 28 = 8$

Per cent means "out of 100". You can use that to write a percentage as a fraction. $\longrightarrow$ $5\% = \dfrac{5}{100}$

To write a fraction as a percentage, find an equivalent fraction with denominator 100. $\longrightarrow$ $\dfrac{3}{10} = \dfrac{30}{100} = 30\%$

To write a percentage as a decimal, divide by 100. $\longrightarrow$ $17\% = 17 \div 100 = 0.17$

Now Try These

1. Jay has $\dfrac{9}{14}$ of a pint of milk in a bottle.

   He pours $\dfrac{2}{7}$ of a pint into a blender to make a milkshake.

   He spills another $\dfrac{3}{28}$ of a pint from the bottle onto the kitchen counter.

   How much milk is left in the bottle?

   $\dfrac{\boxed{}}{\boxed{}}$ of a pint

2. A shoe shop has a sale on. A pair of shoes cost $\dfrac{13}{20}$ of their original price.

   What percentage of the original price of the shoes has been taken off?

   .... %

3. Work out the missing numbers in these calculations.

$$\frac{3}{5} + \frac{\boxed{}}{5} = 2\frac{1}{5}$$

$$\frac{5}{6} \times \boxed{} = \frac{35}{6}$$

$$\frac{\boxed{}}{3} - \frac{4}{9} = \frac{2}{9}$$

$$\frac{\boxed{}}{4} \times 16 = 12$$

4. 200 people go on a boat trip. 65% of them are children.
   How many children are on the boat trip?

   ....

5. A scientist has 3 pet frogs, Ribbo, Croaker and Hoppy. Ribbo weighs $\frac{1}{3}$ kg, Croaker weighs $\frac{3}{18}$ kg and Hoppy weighs $\frac{7}{24}$ kg. Which frog weighs the most?

   ....

6. A postal worker's van is full of items to deliver. $\frac{3}{4}$ of the items are letters, 10% are parcels and the rest are postcards. What proportion of the items in the van are postcards? Give your answer as a decimal.

   ....

An Extra Challenge

Azi's shirts are red, purple, green or pink.
The table shows what fraction of Azi's shirts are each colour. Some of the information is missing.

Red	$\frac{1}{8}$
Purple	
Green	$\frac{1}{2}$
Pink	$\frac{1}{4}$

a) What fraction of Azi's shirts are either red or pink?

b) What fraction of Azi's shirts are purple?

c) Azi has 3 red shirts.
   How many shirts does she have altogether?

Are you 100% confident with fractions and percentages?

Measuring and Time

How It Works

You'll need to know your **unit conversions** to solve measuring and time problems:

Metric	Imperial	Time
1 kilometre (km) = 1000 metres (m)	8 kilometres (km) ≈ 5 miles	1 min = 60 secs
1 metre (m) = 100 centimetres (cm)	1 metre (m) ≈ 3 feet	1 hour = 60 mins
1 centimetre (cm) = 10 millimetres (mm)	5 centimetres (cm) ≈ 2 inches	1 week = 7 days
1 kilogram (kg) = 1000 grams (g)	1 kilogram (kg) ≈ 2 pounds	1 year = 12 months
1 litre (l) = 1000 millilitres (ml)	100 grams (g) ≈ 4 ounces	
	1 litre (l) ≈ 2 pints	

This symbol means 'approximately equal to'.

A problem might involve amounts in different units — make sure you convert them all to the **same units** before you do any calculations with them. Here's an example:

A bowl weighs 300 g. Carl puts 1.2 kg of flour into the bowl.
What is the total mass of the bowl and the flour, in kilograms?

Convert the mass of the bowl to kg. → 1 kg = 1000 g
300 ÷ 1000 = 0.3
So 300 g = 0.3 kg.

Then add the mass of the
flour to the mass of the bowl. → Total mass = 0.3 kg + 1.2 kg = **1.5 kg**

Now Try These

1. Katie is going to the theatre. The diagram shows how she travels there.
   How many kilometres does she travel in total?

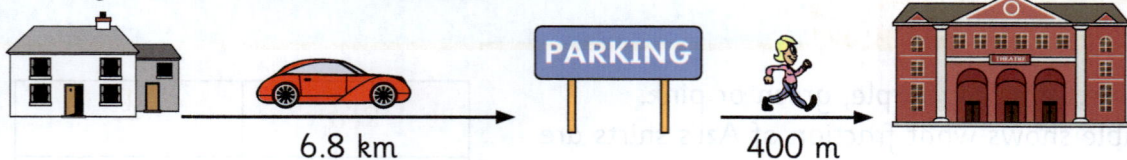

6.8 km   400 m

.... km

2. Arjun's dog is 6 inches tall. His cat is 25 cm tall.
   Approximately how much taller is his cat than his dog, in centimetres?

.... cm

3. It took Zena 4 minutes to work out three sums.
   It took her exactly the same amount of time to work out each sum.
   How many seconds did it take her to do one sum?

.... seconds

4. Nathan has 1.5 litres of orange juice in a bottle. He pours out three glasses of juice so that each glass contains 200 ml. How many millilitres of juice are left in the bottle?

.... ml

5. The track for a sack race is 40 m long. With each jump, Chenda travels 25 cm. Chenda has jumped along half of the track so far. How many times has she jumped?

....

An Extra Challenge

A recipe in metric units for one serving of cheesy pasta is shown below. Use approximate conversions to work out what the recipe would be for **ten people**, in **imperial** units.

Cheesy Pasta for One Person

Pasta   100 g

Cheese   50 g

Milk   250 ml

Cheesy Pasta for Ten People

Pasta   .... pounds

Cheese   .... ounces

Milk   .... pints

Are your measuring skills miles better now?

13

Mountain to Climb

Jez and Jacinda are off up Mega Mountain for a parachute jump, but they keep running into trouble. Follow their path up the mountain, and their jump down, solving the problems on the way. Use your answers to work out at what time they set up camp.

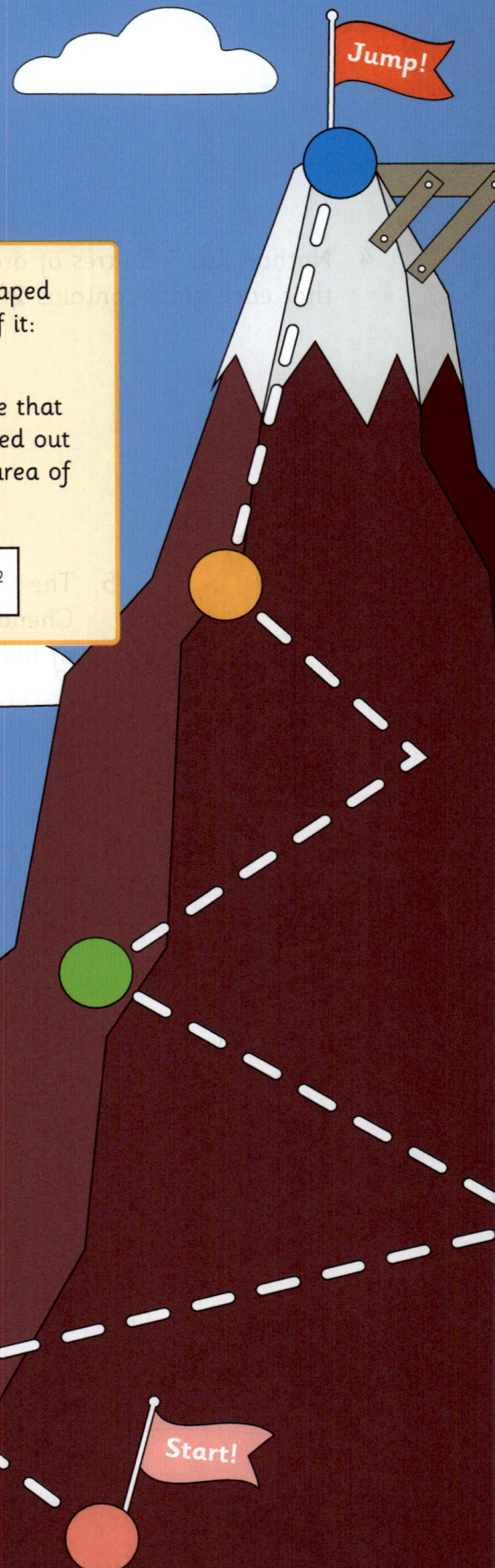

Jump!

Problem 3

The flag is within reach now! But a triangle-shaped piece has been **ripped off**. Here's a diagram of it:

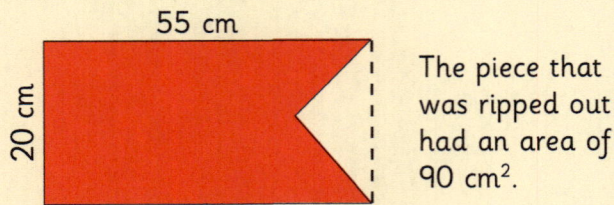

55 cm

20 cm

The piece that was ripped out had an area of 90 cm².

What is the **area** of the remaining flag?

.... cm²

Problem 2

NOT CHOCOLATE

Jez stops at the tuck shop for some snacks.

He buys **8 fruit bars** for **53p each**, then pays with **two £2** coins and **three 10p** coins.

How much does Jez get back in change?

.... p

Problem 1

Something is wrong with Jacinda's compass...

It was pointing North as normal, when suddenly the needle made **3 full turns**, ending up back at North again.

How many degrees did the needle turn?

.... °

Start!

Jez makes a note of the temperature at the peak.

"It was really cold at the peak of the mountain, but as we descended on our jump, it got warmer and warmer.
We fell for **1200 metres**, and it became **3 °C warmer** every **300 metres**."

It was **12 °C** where Jez landed.
What was the temperature at the peak of the mountain?

.... °C

Problem 5

Jacinda describes one of the clouds she saw halfway down:

"One of the clouds had a shape of **equal sides and angles**. Its number of sides was a **single-digit factor of 72**, and **1 less than a square number** — but it wasn't a **prime**."

What shape was the cloud Jacinda is describing?

....

Setting up Camp

Add up the answers to Problems 1-4, and the number of sides of the cloud in Problem 5 to get a **four-digit number**.
Write these into the boxes to find the time Jez and Jacinda finished setting up camp.

Jez and Jacinda set up camp at:

[.........] [.........] : [.........] [.........]

Money

How It Works

Some questions on money will need you to convert between pounds (£) and pence (p). Here's an example for you:

> Chad buys 2 sticker packs for 90p, and gets 10p in change. How much do 12 sticker packs cost? Give your answer in £.

2 sticker packs cost 90p − 10p = 80p, so 1 sticker pack costs 80p ÷ 2 = 40p.

First off, work out the price of one sticker pack.

12 × 40p = 480p, which is 480 ÷ 100 = £4.80

Then multiply it to find the cost of 12 packs, and convert to pounds.

Now Try These

1. Earmuffs are sold at 80p a pair.
   How much change would you get if you paid for...

   a) four pairs of earmuffs with £4?   £ ....

   b) seven pairs of earmuffs with £10?   £ ....

   c) ten pairs of earmuffs with £9.50?   £ ....

2. Curly's Farm sells different kinds of produce.
   Their prices are shown in the table.
   If you buy as many bags of carrots as you can with £20, how much money would you have left?

Produce	Price
Bag of cabbages	£9.45
Bag of potatoes	£6.20
Bag of carrots	£5.90

   £ ....

3. Danny pays for a pair of shoes with a £50 note and gets £22.50 in change.
   The shoes were sold to Danny at half price. What would the shoes cost at full price?

   £ ....

4. At the joke shop, Helena buys 4 packets of gum and two jack-in-the-boxes for £9.20. One packet of gum costs 85p. How much does one jack-in-the-box cost?

£ ....

5. Shabana wants to spend as little as possible on a TV. Below are the normal prices and discounts on three TVs. Circle the one that Shabana should buy.

£1200 25% off!

£2000 ½ off!

£1000 20% off!

6. Peter the potter makes people pottery. It costs £48 to buy 3 vases from Peter. Judit pays for 12 vases with £255. How much change does she get?

£ ....

An Extra Challenge

There's been a robbery at the bank! Luckily, some witnesses can piece together the story. Use their reports to work out the total value of everything the thieves got away with.

= £5500

£2400 = GOLD

One of the thieves grabbed 5 diamonds and £4000 in cash...

...and then another took 9 gold bars...

...but just before they sped off in their van, £1600 spilled out of the back!

Did that all go well? Don't tell any porkies...

17

Angles

How It Works

Angles are measured in degrees (°), and there are four types: **acute**, **right angles**, **obtuse** and **reflex**.

You can draw and measure angles using a protractor.

Angles around a point add up to **360°** and angles on a line add up to **180°**.

360°

180°

360° is a full turn and 180° is a half turn, so 90° is a quarter turn and 270° is a three-quarter turn.

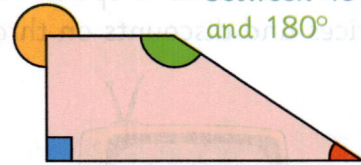

reflex — more than 180°

obtuse — between 90° and 180°

right angle — 90°

acute — less than 90°

Now Try These

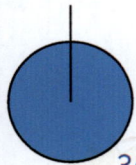

1. Bart used a protractor to measure the angle below, but he wasn't completely accurate. Using your own protractor, work out by how many degrees Bart's measurement is out.

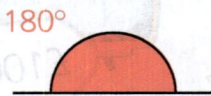

Looks like 36° to me...

Bart is out by ....°

2. Kenzo created this origami shark. Without measuring, work out the missing angles.

...............°

...............°

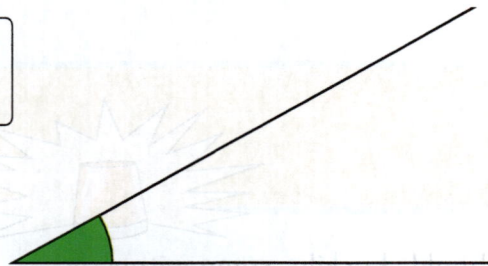

119°
?
?
111°
136°

3. Four identical angles add up to 360°. What type of angle is each angle? How do you know?

....

....

4. Norma starts to spin around in a circle.
   She spins clockwise 45°, then a further 130°, then a further 78°.
   How many more degrees does she need to spin to make a full turn?

   ....°

5. Milla is having a pizza party and wants to slice her pizza up into equal slices.

   a) How many slices would there be if each slice made
      an angle of 45° at the centre of the pizza?

   .... slices

   Six people (including Milla) come to the party in total.
   They each get two equal slices.

   b) What angle does each slice make at the centre of the pizza?

   ....°

6. The Amazing Angletta claims she can fit one of every type of angle
   around a single point. Is she right or wrong? Explain your answer.

   ....

   ....

An Extra Challenge

Something incredible happened at the final of
World's Sharpest Archer... **Team R**, **Team B** and
Team G hit the bullseye with both their arrows!

The judges have decided to award the prize to
the team whose arrows have the largest obtuse
angle between them.

Without measuring, work out which team won,
and by how many degrees.

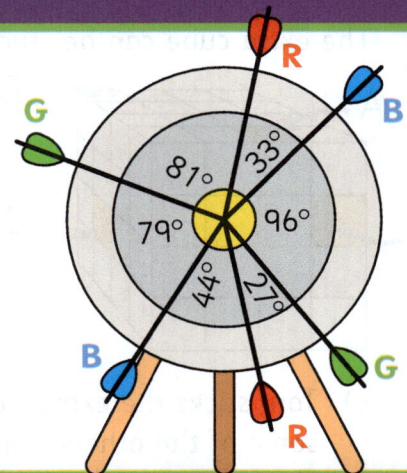

81° 33°
79° 96°
44° 27°

How did that go? Did you get
yourself in a right tangle?

19

Shapes

How It Works

You can solve problems using the properties of shapes.

Regular shapes have equal sides and equal angles.

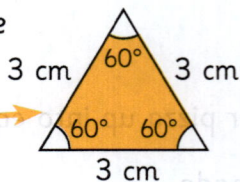

3 cm   60°   3 cm
60°   60°
3 cm

Rectangles have two pairs of equal sides.

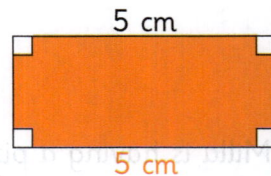

5 cm
5 cm

The top of the rectangle is 5 cm long, so the bottom is 5 cm too.

You can **move** shapes on a grid.

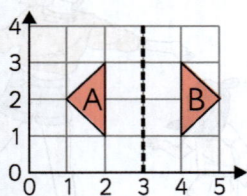

Triangle A has been **reflected** in the mirror line to make triangle B.

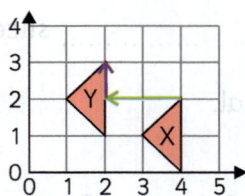

Triangle X has been **translated** 2 squares left and one square up to make triangle Y.

You can show what **3D** shapes look like by drawing them in **2D**.

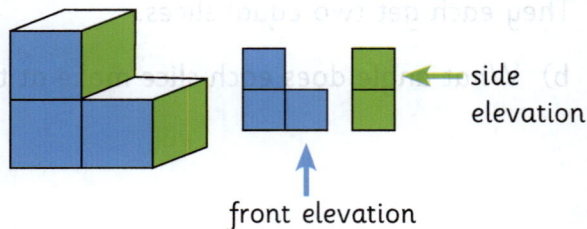

← side elevation

front elevation

Now Try These

1. Johar starts to draw a regular shape.

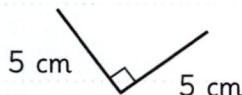

   5 cm   5 cm

   What shape will it be when it's finished? ....

2. Tom makes a cube shape out of smaller cubes, but he has one left over. →
   The extra cube can be stuck to the faces of the small cubes labelled A to D.

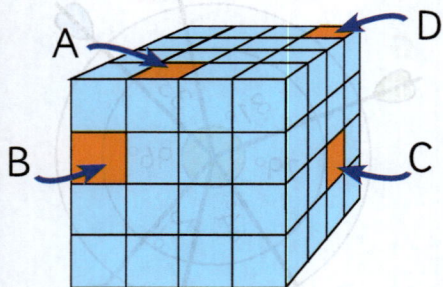

   A   D
   B   C

   a) To which of faces A to D could Tom stick the extra cube so that the shape's front elevation remains the same? ....

   b) To which of faces A to D could Tom stick the extra cube so that the shape's side elevation remains the same? ....

   c) Tom sticks the extra cube on the shape, and removes some of the others. Then he draws the front elevation. →
      How many blocks did he remove? ....

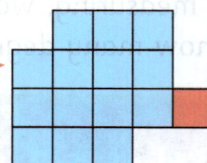

3. Four shapes from the top grid have been translated or reflected to get to their places in the bottom grid.

Fill in the table with the transformations you'd need to use on the bottom grid to return the shapes to their correct places.

If it's a translation, describe it fully. If it's a reflection, draw and label the mirror line on the grid.

Body part	Reflection or translation?	Translation instructions
Body		
Leg		
Neck		
Tail		

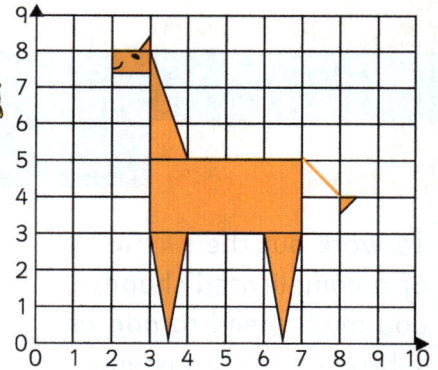

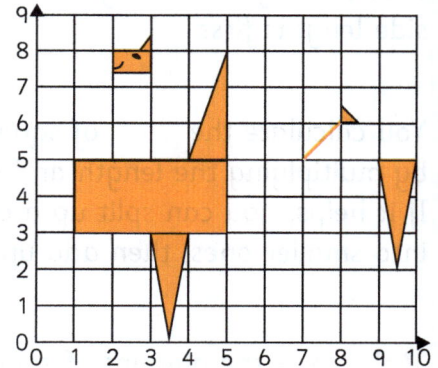

4. Catherine is building a podium out of blocks for a go-kart racing championship. The front elevation of her design is shown below.

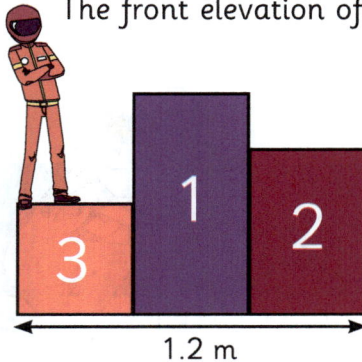

Each block is of equal width. The front of 3rd place is a square. The 1st place block is twice as high as the 3rd place block, and the 2nd place block is $\frac{3}{4}$ of the height of the 1st place block. Work out the dimensions of the front of the 2nd place block.

1.2 m

...........cm by ....cm

An Extra Challenge

Amarjit wants to build a model house like this.

He cuts the shapes that he will need to make it out of card. The shapes are formed from identical squares, rectangles and triangles.

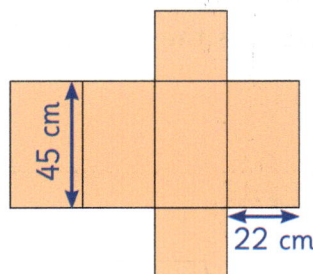

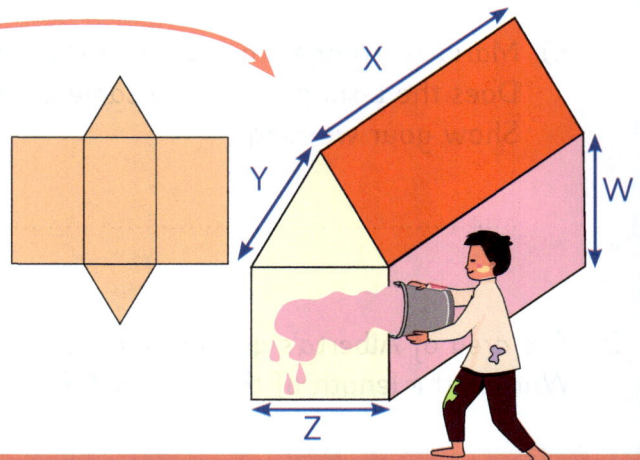

45 cm

22 cm

Can you work out the dimensions of the parts of the house labelled W, X, Y and Z?

X

Y

W

Z

Take a moment to reflect...
How are you shaping up?

Perimeter, Area & Volume

How It Works

To work out the **perimeter** of a complicated shape, you might need to add or subtract to find missing side lengths first.

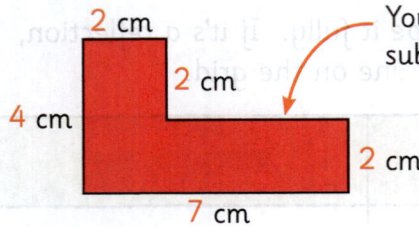

2 cm
2 cm
4 cm
2 cm
7 cm

You'd work this side out with subtraction: 7 − 2 = 5 cm.

So the perimeter is
2 + 2 + 5 + 2 + 7 + 4
= 22 cm.

You calculate the **area** of squares and rectangles by multiplying the length and width together. If it helps, you can split up a complicated shape into smaller ones, then add up their areas.

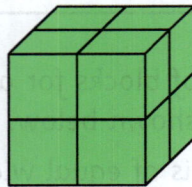

Volume is the amount of space a shape takes up. You can work it out by counting cubes.

There are 8 cubes in the shape, so the volume is 8 cm³.

(1 cube = 1 cm³)

Capacity is the amount a container can hold.

So a container of this size would have a capacity of 8 cm³.

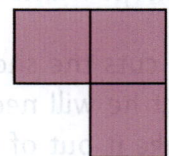

Now Try These

1. Maria makes a rectangle out of three identical square tiles.

   a) What is the perimeter of the rectangle?

   5 cm

   .... cm

   b) Maria rearranges the tiles so they're in an L-shape. Does the L-shape have the same perimeter as the rectangle? Show your working.

   ....

   5 cm

2. The area of Alberta's garden is 72 m².
   What is the length of the short side?

   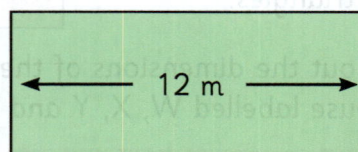
   12 m

   .... m

3. 8 layers like the one on the left are stacked on top of each other to make a tower. The total capacity of the hole in the tower is 16 cm³. What is the volume of one cube?

.... cm³

4. Garth wants to know how much of a wall he has painted.
   He measures some of the lengths of the painted section.
   What is the **area** of the painted section?

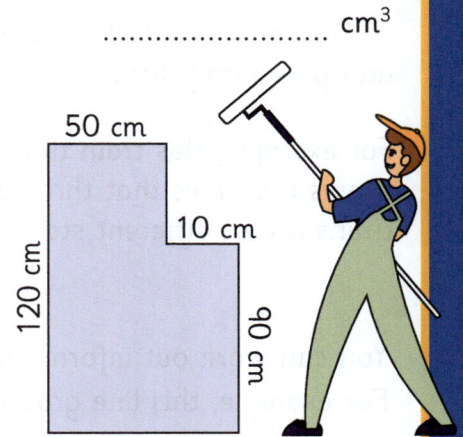

50 cm

10 cm

120 cm

90 cm

.... cm²

5. Wendy the carpenter is building a small desk for one of her customers.
   She needs a rectangular desktop with a short side of 30 cm and a perimeter of 200 cm.
   What should the length of one of the long sides be?

.... cm

An Extra Challenge

Someone has put a hole in the wall. The perimeter of the hole is 400 cm and the long edge of each brick is twice as long as the short edge. Find the dimensions of one brick.

How was that? Is this your
newest area of expertise?

Graphs and Tables

How It Works

Tables are a way of organising and presenting data.

For example, this train timetable shows the times that three different trains are at different stops.

Toots	Wheesh	Chuffa
15:30	16:02	16:49
16:15	16:47	17:34
17:32	18:04	18:51

The last train arrives in Chuffa 1 hour 17 minutes after the one before it.

The train that leaves Toots at 16:15 gets to Wheesh at 16:47.

You can work out information from **line graphs**.
For example, this line graph shows Jason and Sunita climbing a hill.

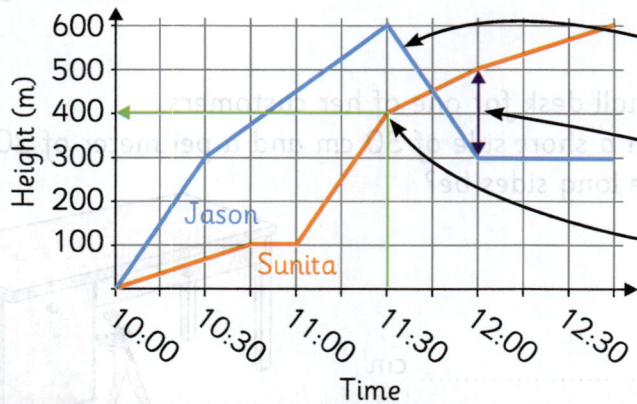

Between 11:30 and 12:00, Jason is climbing down the hill.

At 12:00 Sunita is 500 – 300 = 200 m higher than Jason.

At 11:30 Sunita is at 400 m.

Now Try These

1. Solomon had two types of magic bean. He planted one of each type and recorded their heights at the end of each day in the table below.

Day	1	2	3	4	5	6
Bloomin' Beanstalks (cm)	26	98	159	291	564	1675
Gargantuan Growers (cm)						

Gargantuan Growers

On odd numbered days, I grow 75 cm. On even numbered days I double in height.

a) Using the information above, fill in the table for the Gargantuan Growers.

b) Which beanstalk grew the most in one day?

2. Here is the intergalactic space shuttle timetable, but two times are missing.

a) Shuttles leave Voovam at regular intervals. Fill in the missing time in the timetable.

Voovam	Xargo	Yamuli	Zronkle
05:35	05:50	07:32	10:02
07:35	08:01	09:45	12:05
	10:05	11:18	13:48
11:35	11:59	13:04	

b) How long will it take you to get from Xargo to Zronkle on the 08:01 shuttle?

.... hours .... minutes

c) The 13:04 shuttle takes twice as long as the previous shuttle from Yamuli to Zronkle. Fill in the time the last shuttle arrives in Zronkle.

3. Maisie and Mo competed in the Mud Munchers Extreme obstacle course race, which is 7 km long. The graph below shows their progress during the race.

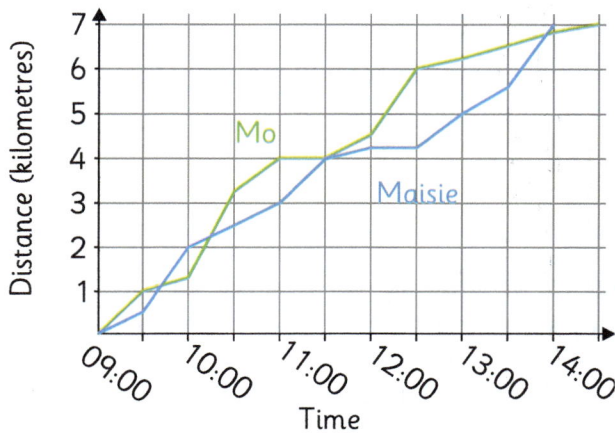

a) Who completed the course first?

....

b) How much further ahead was Mo at 11:00? .... km

c) Mo got stuck at the climbing wall for a while. How long was Mo stuck for?

.... minutes

An Extra Challenge

Izzy sells ice creams on the beach. She records how much money she makes during one day. Match Izzy's thoughts to the correct sections of the graph.

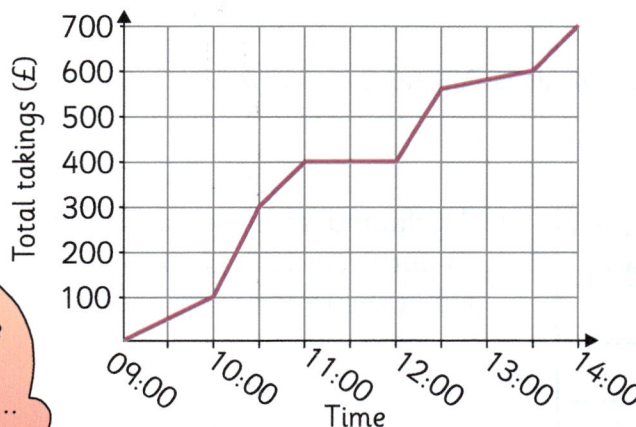

Sales this $\frac{1}{2}$ hour are half the total of the previous 30 minutes.

I made about £40 during the last hour.

Ooh! Here comes the midday rush...

It's raining. Bother! No one wants ice cream in the rain.

I've made twice as much money during the last $\frac{1}{2}$ hour than the whole hour before.

Time to present your feelings about this topic...

25

Mixed Problems

How It Works

Some problems need a **mix** of different skills to solve them. You have to work out what you need to do to find the answer. Have a look at this example:

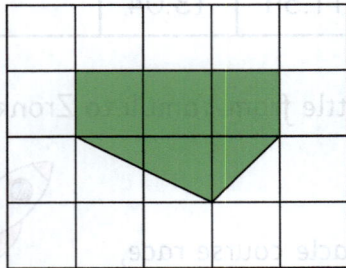

a) Arthur has drawn a plan of his garden. Each square on the grid represents a 5 m by 5 m square in real life. Calculate the area of the garden.

There are $4\frac{1}{2}$ squares shaded in total and each square represents $5 \times 5 = 25$ m². $4 \times 25 = 100$ m² and $\frac{1}{2}$ of 25 is 12.5, so $100 + 12.5 = 112.5$ m² in total.

b) If it takes Arthur 20 minutes to mow 25 m², how long will it take him to mow the whole garden?

You already know that each square is 25 m² and that there are $4\frac{1}{2}$ squares. $20 \times 4 = 80$ and $\frac{1}{2}$ of $20 = 10$, so $80 + 10 = 90$ minutes in total, which is 1 hour 30 minutes.

Now Try These

1. Alysha's mum has asked her to make dinner for the family — 4 people in total. Her instructions, and the amounts she has of some ingredients, are shown below.

There's 1.2 l of gravy in the fridge. It needs 2 minutes per 100 ml to heat up.

Cook the turkey for 20 minutes for every kilogram plus an extra 50 minutes.

You need 140 g of potato per person. The potatoes need $1\frac{1}{2}$ hours in the oven.

Please make dinner for 6 pm. Put the carrots on 20 minutes before it's time to eat.

a) If Alysha cooks all the gravy how much will each person get?

.... ml

b) What quantity of potatoes is Alysha over or under by?

under/over by .... g

c) Alysha makes herself a table so she remembers to put everything on at the right time. Fill in the missing information.

Food item	Time to start cooking
Turkey	
Potatoes	
Carrots	
Gravy	

2. Iniko is decorating one of the walls in his room. He wants to stencil some arrows on the wall and finish the design with some stick-on strips.

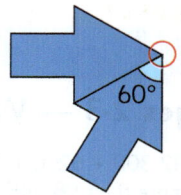

   a) He paints the arrows around a point.
      How many arrows can he fit round the point?

      ....

      60°

   Iniko wants a single line of the stick-on strips to create a border along the wall. His wall is 3.4 m long and each strip costs £4.25.

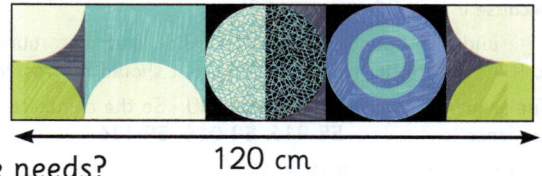

   120 cm

   b) How much will it cost him to buy the strips he needs?

      £ ....

   c) What length of strip will he have left over?

      ....cm

3. Fabian is shopping for cake for his party. There are some offers on at the bakery. How much will it cost him to buy 10 slices of rainbow cake, 3 whole sponge cakes and 1 whole pink strawberry cake?

   80 p per slice

   25% off

   $\frac{1}{2}$ price

   was £10   was £15.50

   £ ....

An Extra Challenge

Mrs Ferris is taking the whole school on an end-of-year trip. There are 433 pupils in the school and 35 teachers, including Mrs Ferris. Mrs Ferris comes up with a way to transport everyone using 12 vehicles in total, with only one spare seat.

How does she do it?

coaches can carry
48 people

cars can carry
5 people

minibuses can carry
16 people

Answers

Pages 2-3 — Working with Numbers

1. 92 300 + 6200 + 120 + 20 + 5 = 98 645, which is 300 more than 98 345. 6200 should be replaced with **5900**, because it is 300 less than 6200.

2. 9.42 and 9.44 round down to 9.4. 9.38 and 9.35 round up to 9.4. 9.34 rounds down to 9.3, so it should be crossed out.

3. The sequence goes up in steps of 100. So the complete sequence is: 58 816, **58 916, 59 016, 59 116,** 59 216.

4. a) Count back 8 °C from 4 °C.
Then count forward 3 °C.
So her butter is **−1 °C**.

$$\underset{-4}{\quad}\quad\underset{-1}{\quad}\underset{0}{\quad}\quad\quad\underset{4}{\quad}$$

   b) Count back in tenths from 8 °C until you get a temperature that doesn't round back up. 7.4 °C rounds down to 7 °C, so the coldest possible temperature is **7.5 °C**.

5. The maximum scores go up in steps of 10 000:
190 000 (Level 5), 200 000 (Level 6), 210 000 (Level 7), 220 000 (Level 8), 230 000 (Level 9), 240 000 (Level 10) and 250 000 (**Level 11**).

An Extra Challenge

−121 − 10 + 30 − 3 − 50 = **−154 m**

Pages 4-5 — Adding and Subtracting

1.
```
  1 5 3 9 0 4          5 13
+ 3 9 1 2 3 4      8 6 5 6 3 7
-----------       - 7 0 1 5 7 6
  5 4 5 1 3 8      ----------
  1   1     8      1 6 4 0 6 1
```

2. Round to the nearest thousand, and add together:
65 000 + 13 000 = **78 000**

3.
```
  2 1
  3 4 . 9 5
- 1 5 . 5 1      So Dr Shrinko is 19.44 cm today.
---------
  1 9 . 4 4      So Trisha is 19.44 − 9.2 = 10.24 cm smaller.
```

4. Subtract to find how many more hot dogs she cooks each year, then add to find how many she will cook this year:
```
    6 6 7 0          2 4 6 7 0
- 1 3 4 1 2        + 1 1 2 5 8
---------          ---------
  1 1 2 5 8          3 5 9 2 8
                          1
```

5.
```
  1 4 . 7 5
  1 3 . 4 6        So the first three runners finished in 43.4 s.
+ 1 5 . 1 9        So the fourth runner's time is
---------          59 − 43.4 = 15.6 s.
  4 3 . 4 0
  1 1 2
```

An Extra Challenge

Year 2124
```
  5 6 7 3 2
+ 1 0 9 0 2
---------
  6 7 6 3 4
  1
```
Year 2125
```
  5 15 5 12 1
  6 7 6 3 4
-     8 0 9 9
---------
  5 9 5 3 5
```
Year 2126
```
  5 9 5 3 5
+ 2 0 5 1 4
---------
  8 0 0 4 9
  1 1
```

Pages 6-7 — Factors, Multiples & Primes

1. Use one number from each of these pairs:
18 or **81**, **27** or **72**, **36** or **63**

2. **1** (= 1² = 1³) and **64** (= 8² = 4³)

3. a) **12** should be crossed out. The missing number is **15**.
   b) **3 and 5**

4. 36 = 6 × 6 and 6 = 3 × 2, so option **C** should be circled.

An Extra Challenge

The only number that meets all four instructions is **63 litres**.

Pages 8-9 — Multiplying and Dividing

1. 1000 pencils come in 1000 ÷ 10 = 100 packs.
So 1000 pencils cost 100 × £2.85 = **£285**.

2. a) 108 ÷ 12 = 9, so 1 bar of chocolate weighs 1080 g ÷ 12 = **90 g**.
   b) 72 ÷ 9 = 8, so one bike weighs 720 kg ÷ 90 = **8 kg**.

3.
```
      1 8 3 r 5
  9 | 1 1 6 7 5 3 2
```
So they could plant the roses in 183 rows of 9, plus another row of 5. So the smallest number of rows is **184**.

4.
```
    2 6 1 8
  ×     4 2
  ---------
    5 2 3 6
  1 0 4 7 2 0
  ---------
  1 0 9 9 5 6  seconds
```

5. 2 weeks = 14 days
```
    3 9 2 4
  ×     1 4
  ---------
  1 5 6 9 6
  3 9 2 4 0
  ---------
  5 4 9 3 6  m
  1   1
```

An Extra Challenge

5 × 12 = 60, so she bought 500 × 12 = 6000 beads. She had 6000 − 70 = 5930 beads left after making the necklace.
```
      7 4 1 r 2
  8 | 5 5 9 3 1 0
```
So she made **741 bracelets**, with **2 beads left over**.

Pages 10-11 — Fractions, Decimals & Percentages

1. $\frac{9}{14} - \frac{2}{7} - \frac{3}{28} = \frac{18}{28} - \frac{8}{28} - \frac{3}{28} = \frac{7}{28}$ (or $\frac{1}{4}$) **of a pint**

2. $1 - \frac{13}{20} = \frac{20}{20} - \frac{13}{20} = \frac{7}{20}$ of the price has been taken off.
So $\frac{7}{20} = \frac{35}{100} = $ **35%** has been taken off.

3. $2\frac{1}{5} = \frac{2 \times 5 + 1}{5} = \frac{11}{5}$, $\frac{11}{5} - \frac{3}{5} = \frac{8}{5}$, so $\frac{3}{5} + \frac{8}{5} = 2\frac{1}{5}$
$\frac{5}{6} \times 7 = \frac{5 \times 7}{6} = \frac{35}{6}$
$\frac{2}{9} + \frac{4}{9} = \frac{6}{9} = \frac{2}{3}$, so $\frac{2}{3} - \frac{4}{9} = \frac{2}{9}$
16 ÷ 4 = 4, and 3 × 4 = 12, so $\frac{3}{4} \times 16 = 12$.

4. 65% = $\frac{65}{100}$, so 65% of 200 = $\frac{65}{100}$ of 200
200 ÷ 100 = 2, 65 × 2 = 130, so $\frac{65}{100}$ of 200 = 130
So there are **130** children on the boat.

5. Ribbo: $\frac{1}{3} = \frac{8}{24}$ kg. Croaker: $\frac{3}{18} = \frac{1}{6} = \frac{4}{24}$ kg. Hoppy: $\frac{7}{24}$ kg.
So **Ribbo** weighs the most.

6. $\frac{3}{4} = 0.75$ and 10% = 10 ÷ 100 = 0.1
The proportion that are postcards is 1 − 0.75 − 0.1 = **0.15**.

An Extra Challenge

a) $\frac{1}{8} + \frac{1}{4} = \frac{1}{8} + \frac{2}{8} = \frac{3}{8}$ are either red or pink.

b) $1 - \frac{1}{8} - \frac{1}{2} - \frac{1}{4} = \frac{8}{8} - \frac{1}{8} - \frac{4}{8} - \frac{2}{8} = \frac{1}{8}$ are purple.

c) $\frac{1}{8}$ of the total number of shirts = 3
So the total number of shirts = 3 × 8 = **24**.

Answers

Pages 12-13 — Measuring and Time

1. 400 m = 400 ÷ 1000 = 0.4 km
   Total distance = 6.8 km + 0.4 km = **7.2 km**

2. 2 inches ≈ 5 cm, so 6 inches ≈ 3 × 5 cm = 15 cm
   So the cat is approximately 25 cm − 15 cm = **10 cm** taller.

3. 4 minutes = 4 × 60 = 240 seconds
   So it took Zena 240 ÷ 3 = **80 seconds** to do one sum.

4. There are 3 × 200 ml = 600 ml of juice in the glasses.
   1.5 litres = 1.5 × 1000 = 1500 ml
   So 1500 ml − 600 ml = **900 ml** are left in the bottle.

5. Length of half of the track = 40 m ÷ 2 = 20 m
   20 m = 20 × 100 = 2000 cm
   There are 4 lots of 25 cm in 100 cm, so there are 8 lots of 25 cm in 200 cm. This means there are 80 lots of 25 cm in 2000 cm. So Chenda has jumped **80** times.

   An Extra Challenge
   Pasta: 100 g × 10 = 1000 g = 1 kg for 10 people.
   1 kg ≈ **2 pounds**
   Cheese: 50 g × 10 = 500 g for 10 people
   100 g ≈ 4 ounces, so 500 g ≈ 5 × 4 = **20 ounces**
   Milk: 250 ml × 10 = 2500 ml = 2.5 litres for 10 people.
   1 litre ≈ 2 pints, so 2.5 litres ≈ 2.5 × 2 = **5 pints**
   (These are approximate conversions — you could get different answers if you use different conversions.)

Pages 14-15 — Mountain to Climb

1. There are 360° in one full turn, so there are 3 × 360° = **1080°** in 3 full turns.

2. 8 fruit bars cost 8 × 53p = 424p = £4.24
   Jez pays with 2 × £2 = £4 and 3 × 10p = 30p, so £4.30 in total. So he gets £4.30 − £4.24 = **6p** change.

3. The area of the rectangle is 55 cm × 20 cm = 1100 cm². The remaining flag has area 1100 cm² − 90 cm² = **1010 cm²**.

4. The temperature rises 3 °C every 300 m for 1200 m.
   1200 m ÷ 300 m = 4, so the temperature rises 4 × 3 °C = 12 °C. It's 12 °C where Jez landed, so it must be 12 °C − 12 °C = **0 °C** at the peak.

5. The shape has equal sides and angles, so it is regular. Single digit factors of 72: 1, 2, 3, 4, 6, 8, and 9. 3 and 8 are one less than a square number, but only 8 isn't prime. The shape is 8-sided, so it must be a **regular octagon**.

6. 1080 + 6 + 1010 + 0 + 8 = 2104.
   So Jez and Jacinda finish setting up camp at **21:04**.

Pages 16-17 — Money

1. a) 4 × 80p = 320p = £3.20, and £4 − £3.20 = **£0.80**
   b) 7 × 80p = 560p = £5.60, and £10 − £5.60 = **£4.40**
   c) 10 × 80p = 800p = £8, and £9.50 − £8 = **£1.50**

2. 3 × £5.90 = £17.70, but 4 × £5.90 = £23.60, so you can only buy 3 bags of carrots with £20.
   You would then have £20 − £17.70 = **£2.30** left.

3. The shoes cost Danny £50 − £22.50 = £27.50. This is half price, so at full price they would cost 2 × £27.50 = **£55**.

4. 4 packets of gum cost 4 × 85p = 340p = £3.40, so two jack-in-the-boxes cost £9.20 − £3.40 = £5.80.
   So one jack-in-the-box costs £5.80 ÷ 2 = **£2.90**.

5. 25% = $\frac{1}{4}$, and $\frac{1}{4}$ of £1200 = £1200 ÷ 4 = £300, so the first TV costs £1200 − £300 = £900.
   $\frac{1}{2}$ of £2000 = £2000 ÷ 2 = £1000, so the second TV costs £1000.
   20% = $\frac{1}{5}$, and $\frac{1}{5}$ of £1000 = £1000 ÷ 5 = £200, so the third TV costs £1000 − £200 = £800. This is the cheapest of the three, so the **third TV** should be circled.

6. 12 ÷ 3 = 4, so 12 vases cost 4 × £48 = £192.
   So Judit gets £255 − £192 = **£63** in change.

   An Extra Challenge
   In total, the thieves got away with 5 diamonds, 9 gold bars and £4000 − £1600 = £2400 in cash.
   5 diamonds = 5 × £5500 = £27 500, and
   9 gold bars = 9 × £2400 = £21 600, so in total they got away with £27 500 + £21 600 + £2400 = **£51 500**

Pages 18-19 — Angles

1. The angle is 30°, so Bart is out by 36° − 30° = **6°**

2. 180° − 119° = **61°**
   360° − 111° − 136° = **113°**

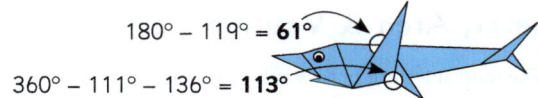

3. Each angle is identical, so they are each 360° ÷ 4 = 90°. Right angles are 90°, so each angle is a **right angle**.

4. A full turn is 360°. Norma spins 45° + 130° + 78° = 253°. So she needs to spin 360° − 253° = **107°** more.

5. a) 8 × 45° = 360°, so there would be **8 slices**.
   b) There are 2 × 6 = 12 slices in total, so each slice makes 360° ÷ 12 = **30°** at the centre of the pizza.

6. A reflex angle is more than 180°, and a right angle is 90°, so she'll need to fit an acute angle and an obtuse angle into 360° − 180° − 90° = 90°. But obtuse angles are more than 90°, so Angletta is **wrong**.

   An Extra Challenge
   Team R: 33° + 96° + 27° = 156°
   Team B: 96° + 27° + 44° = 167°
   Team G: 27° + 44° + 79° = 150°
   So **Team B** won by 167° − 156° = **11°**.

Pages 20-21 — Shapes

1. Every side will be 5 cm in length, and every angle will be a right angle. So the finished shape will be a **square**.

2. a) If it was stuck to A or D, it would add a square to the top of the front elevation. If it was stuck to C, it would add a square to the right side of the front elevation. So the answer is **B**.
   b) If it was stuck to A or D, it would add a square to the top of the side elevation. If it was stuck to B, it would add a square to the side of the side elevation. So the answer is **C**.
   c) He has removed the entire bottom right row, and the entire top left row. That's 4 + 4 = **8 blocks** in total.

Answers

3.

Body part	Reflection or translation?	Translation instructions
Body	**Translation**	**2 squares right**
Leg	**Translation**	**3 squares left, 2 squares down**
Neck	**Reflection**	
Tail	**Reflection**	

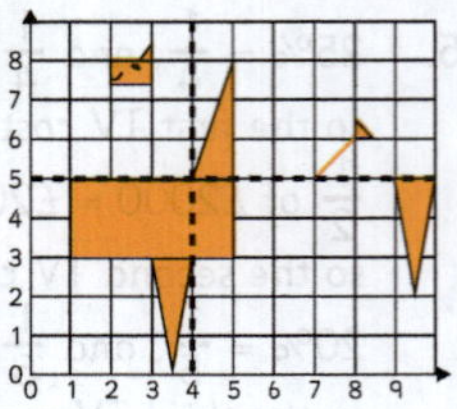

4. Each block is 1.2 m ÷ 3 = 0.4 m = 40 cm wide. Because it's a square, the 3rd place block is 40 cm tall. So the 1st place block is 2 × 40 cm = 80 cm tall, and the 2nd place block is $\frac{3}{4}$ × 80 cm tall. 80 cm ÷ 4 = 20 cm and 20 cm × 3 = 60 cm, so the 2nd block is **40 cm by 60 cm**.

An Extra Challenge

The long edge of each rectangle is 45 cm, and the short edge of each rectangle is 22 cm. The squares match up with the short edges, so their sides are also 22 cm. The triangles match up with the squares, so their sides are 22 cm as well. So, W is **22 cm**, X is **45 cm**, Y is **22 cm** and Z is **22 cm**.

Pages 22-23 — Perimeter, Area & Volume

1. a) The long sides are both 3 × 5 = 15 cm, and the short sides are 5 cm.
So the perimeter is 5 + 15 + 5 + 15 = **40 cm**.
b) The perimeter is 5 + 5 + 5 + 5 + 10 + 10 = 40 cm.
So **yes**, it does have the same perimeter.

2. Area = long side × short side, so 72 = 12 × short side.
So the short side = 72 ÷ 12 = **6 m**.

3. There are 8 layers, so the capacity of the hole is the same as the volume of 8 cubes. So one cube is 16 ÷ 8 = **2 cm³**.

4. Split the shape up into two rectangles:

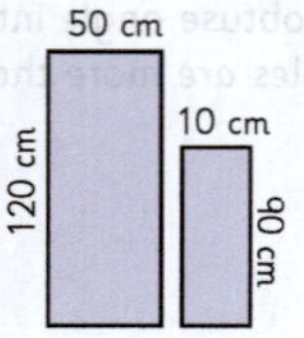

Area of first rectangle:
50 × 120 = 6000 cm²
Area of second rectangle:
10 × 90 = 900 cm²
Total area = 6000 + 900 = **6900 cm²**

5. The lengths of the short sides add up to 30 + 30 = 60 cm. The perimeter is 200 cm, so the long sides need to be 200 − 60 = 140 cm in total. There are 2 long sides, so 1 long side is 140 ÷ 2 = **70 cm**.

An Extra Challenge

The perimeter of the hole is made up from short sides, long sides (which are the same as two short sides), and halves of long sides (which are the same as one short side).
So count the amount of 'short sides' that make up the hole:
40 short sides = 400 cm, so one short side is 400 ÷ 40 = 10 cm. So one brick is **10 cm by 20 cm**.

Pages 24-25 — Graphs and Tables

1. a)

Day	1	2	3	4	5	6
Bloomin' Beanstalks (cm)	26	98	159	291	564	1675
Gargantuan Growers (cm)	75	150	225	450	525	1050

b) **Bloomin' Beanstalks** (from 564 cm to 1675 cm)

2. a) Shuttles leave Voovam every 2 hours. So the missing time is 2 hours after 07:35, which is **09:35**.
b) The 08:01 shuttle gets you to Zronkle at 12:05. So the journey is **4 hours and 4 minutes** long.
c) The previous shuttle took 2.5 hours, so this one will arrive 2 × 2.5 hours = 5 hours after 13:04.
So the missing time is **18:04**.

3. a) The course is 7 km long, and Maisie reaches 7 km first.
b) At 11:00, Mo was 4 km along the course, and Maisie was 3 km along the course. So Mo was 4 − 3 = **1 km** ahead.
c) The flat part of the graph shows where Mo is stuck. It goes from 11:00 to 11:30, so Mo is stuck for **30 minutes**.

An Extra Challenge

Sales **from 10:30 and 11:00** (£100) were half the total from 10:00 to 10:30 (£200).
Izzy made about £40 **between 12:30 and 13:30**.
The 'midday rush' was **from 12:00 to 12:30**.
It rained **from 11:00 to 12:00**.
Izzy made twice as much **from 10:00 to 10:30** (£200) as she did from 9:00 to 10:00 (£100).

Pages 26-27 — Mixed Problems

1. a) 1000 × 1.2 l = 1200 ml. There are 4 people in total, so each person will get 1200 ml ÷ 4 = **300 ml**.
b) 140 g × 4 = 560 g. Alysha has 0.5 kg × 1000 = 500 g, so she is **under by 60 g**.
c)

Food item	Time to start cooking	
Turkey	**4:00 pm**	20 min per kg + 50 min: 20 min × 3.5 = 70 min, 70 min + 50 min = 120 min = 2 hours before 6 pm
Potatoes	**4:30 pm**	1.5 hours before 6 pm
Carrots	**5:40 pm**	20 min before 6 pm
Gravy	**5:36 pm**	12 lots of 100 ml of gravy, so 2 × 12 = 24 min before 6 pm

2. a) There are 360° around a point, so Iniko can fit 360° ÷ 60° = **6 arrows** around a point.
b) 120 cm ÷ 100 = 1.2 m. Iniko needs to buy 3 strips to cover 3.4 m, since 2 strips only cover 2 × 1.2 m = 2.4 m while 3 strips cover 3 × 1.2 m = 3.6 m.
So it will cost 3 × £4.25 = **£12.75**.
c) 3.6 m − 3.4 m = 0.2 m, which is 0.2 m × 100 = **20 cm**.

3. 10 slices of rainbow cake: 10 × 80p = 800p = £8
3 sponge cakes: 25% of £10 = $\frac{1}{4}$ of £10 = £10 ÷ 4 = £2.50, so 1 sponge cake costs £10 − £2.50 = £7.50.
3 × £7.50 = £22.50
1 pink strawberry cake: half of £15.50 = £15.50 ÷ 2 = £7.75
Total cost: £8 + £22.50 + £7.75 = **£38.25**

An Extra Challenge

There are 433 + 35 = 468 people in total.
10 coaches would carry 10 × 48 = 480 people, leaving 12 empty seats. So Mrs Ferris can only use **9 coaches**.
9 × 48 = 432, so there are 468 − 432 = 36 people left.
2 × 16 = 32 and 1 × 5 = 5, so if Mrs Ferris uses **2 minibuses** and **1 car**, she'll fit everyone and have 1 seat left over.

MPFPS5Q21